EARTH'S NATURAL DISASTERS

SCARY TSUNAMIS

Jane Katirgis and Michele Ingber Drohan

Enslow PUBLISHING

Words to Know

debris—Pieces of wood, glass, stone, and other materials left after a disaster.

disturbance—A sudden movement that upsets something that is usually still.

earthquake—When the crust of the earth shakes as a result of two plates running into each other.

epicenter—The place on the ground right above where an earthquake happens.

eruption—The spewing of gases, ash, and molten rock from a crack in the earth's crust.

evacuate—To leave an area immediately because it is not safe.

meteorite—A rock from space that has survived the trip through the earth's atmosphere and lands on the earth.

seismograph—An instrument that measures movement in the earth's crust.

tide—The rise and fall of the surface of the ocean.

tsunami—A series of waves caused by a disturbance in the earth's crust in or near the ocean.

wavelength— The distance between two waves in a series of waves.

CONTENTS

Tsunami waves are not the type people surf on. They are more like walls of water.

1

WALL OF WATER

When you think of an ocean wave, you probably imagine the ones that allow you to enjoy surfing and bodyboarding. **Tsunami** waves are not like normal ocean waves made by the wind. Instead, tsunami waves form because of a **disturbance** in or near the ocean.

Tsunami waves can move as fast as 600 miles (966 km) per hour. When a tsunami reaches the coast, the waves can be as high as 100 feet (30.5 m). Usually a tsunami does not look like a big wave. It looks like a huge wall of water moving forward.

2

Tsunami Science

Many people used to call tsunamis tidal waves. But tidal wave is the wrong name. Tsunamis are not affected by the **tides**. Instead, tsunamis are caused by **earthquakes** that occur near or on the ocean floor. Most earthquakes happen because the plates in the earth's crust bump into each other. Because the force of an earthquake is very strong, it pushes large amounts of water to the surface. This is what creates a tsunami. Tsunamis can also form after the **eruption** of a volcano, a landslide, or the crash of a **meteorite** from space.

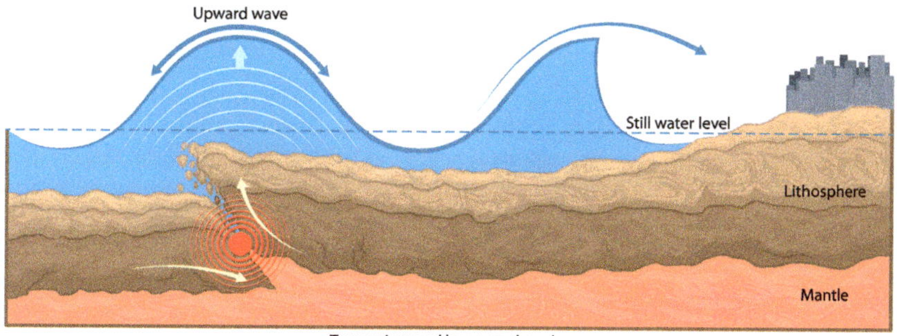

Tsunami caused by an earthquake

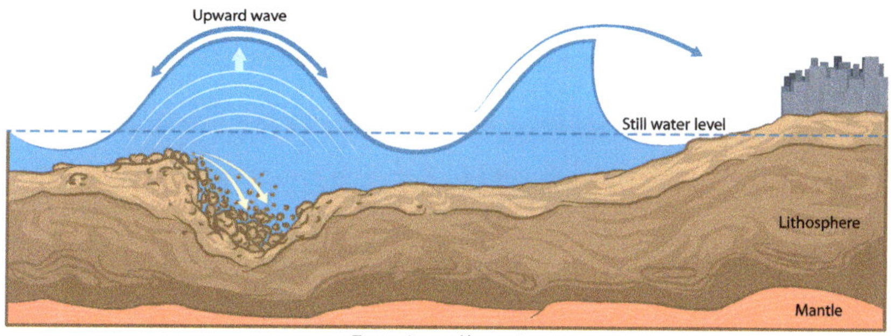

Tsunami caused by erosion

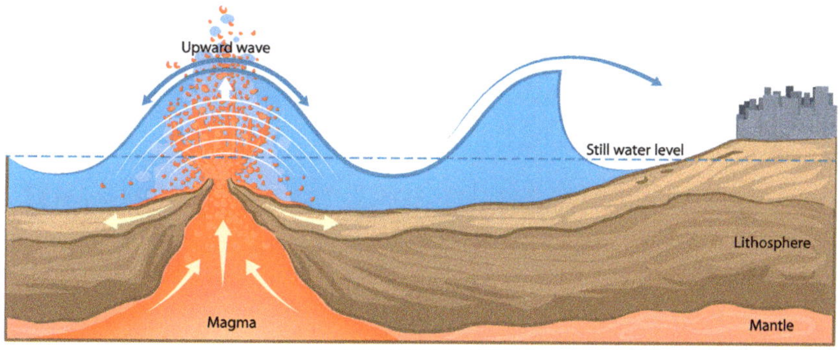

Tsunami caused by the volcano

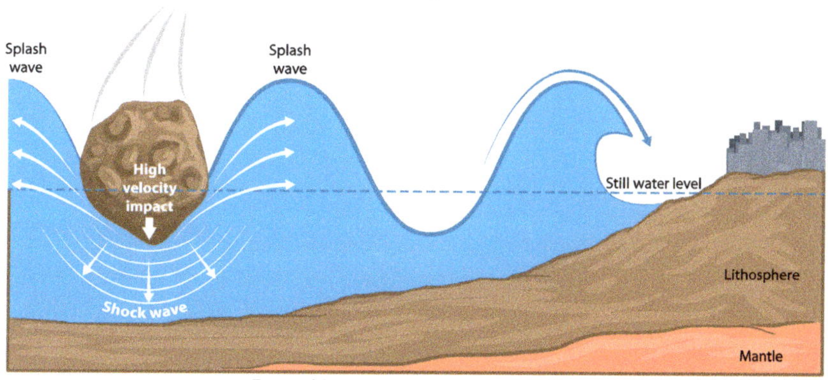

Tsunami (Mega tsunami) caused by falling meteors

What Makes Tsunami Waves Different?

The distance between two waves is called a **wavelength**. The wavelengths of ocean waves that are caused by the wind are usually only 30 to 60 feet (9 to 18 m) long. But the waves of a tsunami can have a wavelength of more than 300 miles (483 km). When the tsunami is in deep water, the waves are only a few feet high. A tsunami could pass under a ship in the middle of the ocean and no one on the ship would notice it. When the wavelength is very long, a tsunami can travel fast. It can move across a whole ocean in less than a day. But when the tsunami reaches shallow water, it slows down. The wavelength of the tsunami gets shorter and shorter until one giant wave is formed.

A tsunami safety sign directs people to move to a safe area.

3

The Power of a Tsunami

A tsunami can cause a lot of damage to the land and people. Even though it slows down when it reaches the land, a tsunami still has a lot of power. In fact, a tsunami is so powerful that it can move large rocks, boats, and cars. A tsunami floods an area and destroys the land. It pulls sand and plant life from the beach. Tsunamis destroy homes and other nearby buildings. Many people don't understand how strong and fast a tsunami can be. Some people have been killed while trying to see a tsunami as it hit shore.

A tsunami in Indonesia caused terrible damage to these homes.

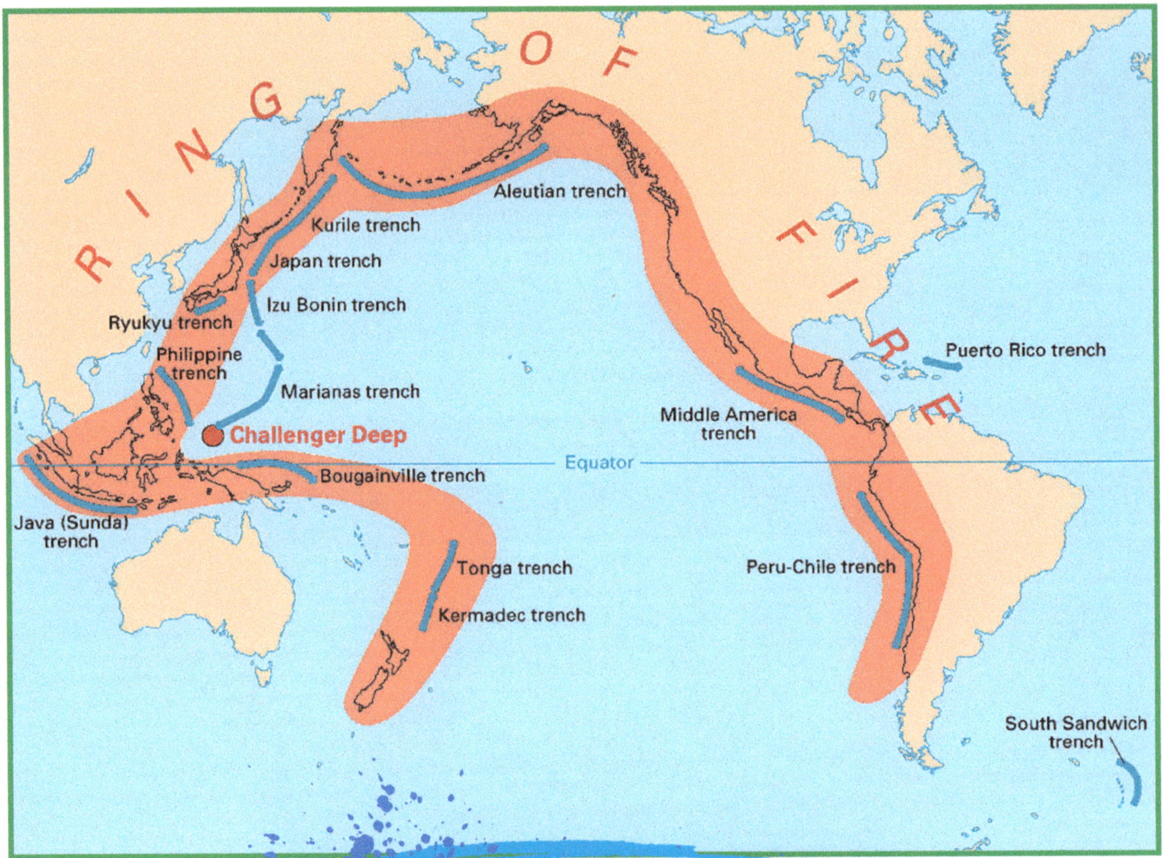

The Ring of Fire includes volcanoes around and under the Pacific Ocean.

Tsunamis Around the World

Tsunamis can happen in every ocean in the world. But they form most often in places around and under the Pacific Ocean because many volcanoes and earthquakes occur there. There are so many volcanoes in this area that it has been named the Ring of Fire.

Scientists from different countries around the Ring of Fire have come together to warn people of tsunamis. Japan and Hawaii are part of this system because over the years they have been hit by many tsunamis.

4

WARNING!

The first Tsunami Warning Center was formed in 1949 after an earthquake near Alaska caused a tsunami that devastated the far away Hawaiian island of Hilo. Now called the Pacific Tsunami Warning Center (PTWC), the organization watches for earthquakes large enough to cause tsunamis. Earthquakes are measured with **seismographs**. If an earthquake happens, the PTWC sends out a watch. During a tsunami watch, information is given to people by radio and television.

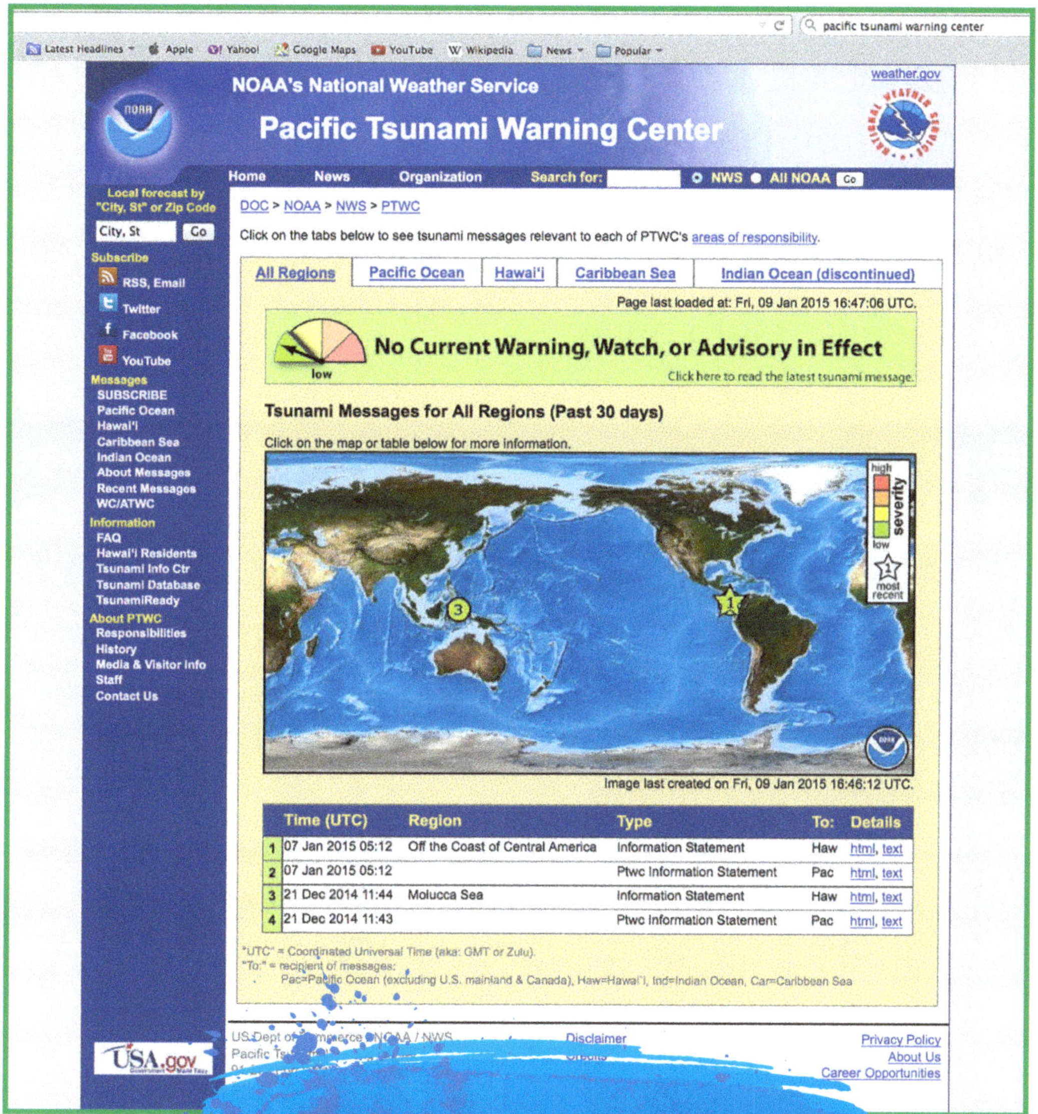

The PTWC Web site tells of earthquake and tsunami dangers.

The PTWC looks at the waves and water level near the **epicenter** of the earthquake to see if a tsunami has formed. If a tsunami has formed, a warning is given. A tsunami warning tells people to **evacuate** right away.

The Christmas Tsunami

It was December 26, 2004. Many families and friends around the world were enjoying the holiday season. But people in Indonesia were about to experience something devastating.

A massive earthquake struck under the ocean near the coast of the island of Sumatra. Its magnitude measured 9.0 on the Richter scale! The shaking ground caused killer waves. The waves sounded like roaring jet engines. One after the other, the waves headed toward land. A total of 227,898 people died in this disaster.

Indonesians pray for the victims of the Indian Ocean tsunami the day before its tenth anniversary.

5

Earthquakes and Tsunamis

Sometimes a tsunami is caused by a nearby earthquake. These are called local tsunamis. Other times, an earthquake happens far away and a tsunami travels hundreds of miles across the ocean.

In 1960, there was an earthquake near Chile. Fifteen minutes after the earthquake happened, a tsunami destroyed the area. Thousands of people died. The tsunami traveled to the other side of the ocean and hit Hawaii fifteen hours later. Sixty-one

In Japan, a tsumani wave caused by an earthquake destroys everything in its path.

more people died. Since then, warning systems have helped save people. But even with a warning, it is hard to save people from local tsunamis because they happen so quickly.

Japan's Tsunami of March 2011

Twenty feet (6 m) below the ocean, an earthquake struck Japan. The shaking lasted for six minutes. The PTWC jumped into action. Warning: A tsunami is on the way! One hour after the massive earthquake, the tsunami hit land. The coast of Japan saw wave after wave. Each wave was higher than 30 feet (9 m).

After the disaster, more than six million homes had no electricity. One million homes had no drinking water. Years later, debris from the tsunami continued to wash up on the beaches, even as far away as North America.

Tsunami waves crash into this Japanese neighborhood.

Debris washed ashore after the tsunami in Japan.

Measuring a Tsunami

You would not want to try to measure the height of a tsunami as it is happening, but experts have found other ways to measure how high the waves are. The maximum height of a tsunami is called a run-up. Experts find the run-up by looking at the **debris** left over from the tsunami. Depending on where the debris is laying, it's possible to figure out how high a wave must have been. Scientists also look at plants and trees that were killed by the salt from the ocean water. Experts do this so they can make evacuation maps. These maps tell people if they are in danger when a tsunami warning is made.

6

Tsunami Safety and the Future

When there is a tsunami warning, it is very important for you to quickly evacuate the area. Listen to the radio or watch the television to find out what to do and where to go. If the earthquake that caused the tsunami is far away, you will have time to move to a safe place. But if the tsunami is local, you may only have a few minutes to escape. If you live near a coast, move to higher ground right away if you feel an earthquake. Don't return home until the experts say it's safe.

Having an evacuation plan makes it easier to know what to do when disaster strikes.

What to Expect

How many tsunamis can we expect in the future? As many as two local tsunamis happen every year. And if experts can predict tsunamis, they can warn people early and give them more time to escape.

Tsunami Warning Buoys

DART (Deep-ocean Assessment and Reporting of Tsunamis) stations include buoys and seafloor sensors. This buoy, shown floating on the water's surface in the photo at right, records changes in pressure measured at the ocean floor. The United States currently has more than thirty of these stations in the Pacific Ocean, the Atlantic Ocean, and the Caribbean Sea. Other countries, including Indonesia, Chile, Thailand, and Australia, have also added these buoys to their tsunami warning systems.

TEWS
UNAMI
TS1

In Indonesia, a scientist conducts a tsunami drill.

Once a tsunami has formed, experts know when it will reach land. But scientists are trying to find a way to tell if a tsunami is going to form even before it has. They use instruments to record movements on the ocean floor. By recording movements, they hope to learn more about these giant waves. The more scientists know about tsunamis, the safer people around the world will be.

Learn More

Books

Gullo, Arthur. *Tsunamis*. New York: Cavendish Square Publishing, 2015.

Kostigen, Thomas. *Extreme Weather: Surviving Tornadoes, Sandstorms, Hailstorms, Blizzards, Hurricanes, and More!* Washington, D.C.: National Geographic Children's Books, 2014.

Simon, Seymour. *Seymour Simon's Extreme Oceans.* San Francisco: Chronicle Books, 2013.

Web Sites

ngkids.co.uk/did-you-know/tsunamis

Dive in and explore tsunamis.

tsunami.noaa.gov/kids.html

Link to videos, activities, safety, and science facts about tsunamis.

INDEX

Published in 2016 by Enslow Publishing, LLC.
101 W. 23rd Street, Suite 240, New York, NY 10011

Library of Congress Cataloging-in-Publication Data
Katirgis, Jane, author.
Scary tsunamis / Jane Katirgis and Michele Ingber Drohan.
pages cm. — (Earth's natural disasters)
Summary: "Discusses the science behind [tsunamis] and what to do to stay safe from them"—Provided by publisher.
Audience: 8+
Audience: Grades 4 to 6
Includes bibliographical references and index.
ISBN 978-0-7660-6807-0 (library binding)
ISBN 978-0-7660-6805-6 (pbk.)
ISBN 978-0-7660-6806-3 (6-pack)
1. Tsunamis—Juvenile literature. 2. Tsunami hazard zones—Juvenile literature. I. Drohan, Michele Ingber, author. II. Title.
GC221.5.K38 2015
551.46'37—dc23

2015008031

Printed in the United States of America

To Our Readers: We have done our best to make sure all Web site addresses in this book were active and appropriate when we went to press. However, the author and the publisher have no control over and assume no liability for the material available on those Web sites or on any Web sites they may link to. Any comments or suggestions can be sent by e-mail to customerservice@enslow.com.

Photo Credits: AFP/Getty Images, p. 19, 28; A.S. Zain/Shutterstock.com, p. 11; © AP Images, pp. 1, 21, 27; EpicStockMedia/Shutterstock.com (chapter openers and back matter backgrounds); Getty Images AsiaPac/ Getty Images News/Getty Images, p. 17; Jamie Farrant/Digital Vision Vectors (caption boxes); LSkywalker/ Shutterstock.com, p. 7; shannonstent/Vetta/Getty Images, p. 4; Pixsooz/Shutterstock.com, p. 25; think4photop/ Shutterstock.com, p. 9; traffic_analyzer/Digital Vision Vectors/Getty Images (page folios); U.S. Geological SurveyDepartment of the Interior/USGS/Reston, VA, p.12; yankane/Shutterstock.com, p. 22.

Cover Credits: © AP Images (tsunami damage); EpicStockMedia/Shutterstock.com (background); traffic_ analyzer/Digital Vision Vectors/Getty Images (series icon).